Reflections of Life

A Selection of Poetry

Suzanne Hobson

Published by

CGW

2010

Reflections of Life

First Edition – March 2010

ISBN 978-0-9565358-0-1

CGW Publishing 2010

© Suzanne Hobson 2010

Published by:

CGW Publishing
B 1502
PO Box 15113
Birmingham
B2 2NJ

Reflections of Life

Serenity...1

The Magnificent Tree.......................................5

Celtic Moods...9

Daydream...13

A Fairground Attraction.................................17

In Loving Memory of my Grandad, Edward................19

Autumn...21

Christmas Time...25

A Little Sunshine...27

Frozen Image...29

Golden Sands...33

July to September...35

My Unborn Child...41

Rainbows..47

Romantic Dinner..49

Summer is here at last!....................................51

Summer Rain 55

The Fifth of November....................................59

The Demon of the Drink!...............................63

Wedding Day..67

Tranquil Bliss..69

Up and Away!...73

Lost In Thought..79

Last Sleep Poem?..85

Our Love..89

Who You Are...91

Forbidden?..95

Awake...97

Time..101

Winter Nights..105

War Destruction and Peace.............................109

Think Positively!..113

Poppies...119

Peaceful Waters...123

Good Friends...127

Dear Santa..129

An April Day – Farewell Grandad....................133

My personal, everyday life experiences have inspired me to write this book... from my heart.

For my family and friends who have given me love, support and much encouragement.

For my partner, Paul, my muse, who has helped me to trust and believe in so many beautiful things again. You are very special to me and I love you with all my heart.

For my parents, Alan and Joan, who have supported me through the good and bad times, for which I am forever grateful. I love you both very dearly.

For my Grandad, who would have been extremely proud.

And for my special friends, Stevie and Peter, for helping me publish this book. Without you both, my dream would not have come true.

Love, Suzanne

Serenity

My thoughts are far away

The tranquil music engulfs me

Trickling water

Birdsong, and forest calls

Like nature's whispers amidst these
feelings and song

Where no words are sung

They don't need to

I feel the place

I know where it lies

Deep in my sub-consciousness

My mind calling to me

Bathing me in tunes

I am AWAKE

But craving SLEEP

To carry me amidst the forest calls

I lie here ALONE

Yet I feel your touch caressing like the
    breeze

Calming me

Aiding for sleep to wash over me

It comes to me like the sea's ocean's
    wave

The melodies take me

Relax me

As my eyes close

My body drifts

As does my mind

Uncontrollably, it takes me on an
    unknown journey

Through my soul

Through a time I don't know

The waves crashing down

The trickling sounds from the music
    surround ME

I am submerged

Unafraid

And loved by YOU

The Magnificent Tree

You are situated tall and proud

Amongst the forest in a crowd

Your branches reach up to the sky

Hovering above you birds they fly

Leafy green shades shelter below

Years go by you carry on to grow

If only you could speak -

What information would you leak?

You are old and you are wise -

If only, you had eyes...

Or ears absorbing all nature's things

To hear all animals the birds to sing?

Your textured bark like leather

As you stand tall in all weather

Autumn and winter comes around

Scatters your leaves to the ground

Now all naked and bare you stand

But still magnificent tall and grand

A longing for spring when leaves of new

To grace your branches instead of dew

As you have done since your birth

Continuing your existence on this earth

You will be here long after I've gone

Like the circle of life we carry on...

Celtic Moods

Celtic Music softly plays as it messes
    with my moods

And in my heart and soul turmoil of
    thoughts they brood

Feelings of loneliness are lost like on a
    planet of bleak

As I lie here thinking of nothing a tear
    rolls down my cheek

Memories of a second home - a land of
    fields of green

Almost in the depth of the melodies the
    places I have seen

Harp and acoustic plays sweet harmonic
    voice alone

The lyrics in the song remind me of
    places of that home

Fire burns melodies absorb sensations
    in my heart

Whilst I lie here thinking of my loved
    one as we're apart

A place, a feeling I want to share as
    sometimes I hide

Enriches my everlasting soul with
    goodness deep inside

My love overwhelms me as I picture
    your kind face

Knowing one day you'll share my
    feeling and see my special place

Daydream

If I could be anywhere -

where would I be?

At this moment in time -

on a boat on the sea!

Where would I be travelling -

where would I end?

Maybe somewhere hot

with a couple of friends!

What would I be doing -

something to entertain?

Chilling with some drinks

and ordering again!

Would the sun be warm

shining upon my face?

Yes and I would be taking it
easy at a slow pace!
Would there be lots to do
and plenty to see?
Many excursions for my
friends and me!
Will I bathe in the sea and
splash and have fun?
In the warm water
as it glistens from the sun!
If only this was real and
I was actually there?
But it's raining in England -
life is so unfair!

A Fairground
Attraction

Ghost train screeches and squeals

The turning of the Ferris wheel

Palms read and fortune tells

The horses on the carousel

Shoot tin cans and try your luck

Dart a card and hook a duck

The waltzer car quickly spins

Win a prize from the lucky bin

Gravity wall and roller-coaster mouse

Funny mirrors and haunted house

Bumper and dodgems bump and collide

The fairground is full of rides

Hot dogs and candy floss smells

Musical melodies and chiming bells

In this clear dark night

Which is lit with fairy lights

A magnificent distraction

Is this Fairground Attraction

*In Loving Memory of
my Grandad, Edward*

Feels like time has stood still as you leave

All of us together to mourn and grieve

No one can replace you – this void an empty
hole

But left is your touch – imprinted upon our
souls

No more suffering – no more pain

You have met up with Grandma again

I will like others remember you, in many ways

Not just for now – but always

You will be the pretty flowers, the honey bee

All of nature's things that you loved to see

You will be the black velvet sky at night

That twinkling star shining bright

I will remember the holidays we had

It warms my heart makes me happy not sad

Remembering our loss as you are laid to rest we
weep

But pray God keeps you safe whilst you are
asleep

Autumn

Evenings are drawing in and
the temperatures drop cold
Autumn colours of rusty browns
greens and gold

From their branch they fall
leaves shrivelled and dead
Birds fly to their nest
early to rise and early to bed

Thundery skies threatens above
to everything below
Air is cool the sky dark
the wind then starts to blow

Lightning begins to strike
and loud thunder claps
Rain starts to pour down
Like water from a tap

Leaves fly up and around
in the midst of the gale
Coming down in sheets
the rain then turns to hail

Hoping for a clear Autumn day
with sunny and blue skies
For today has turned into night
we wait for a new morning to rise

Christmas Time

Children and adults singing carols at the door

Collecting pennies for charity and the poor

Outside the world is white and covered all in snow

Inside a happy couple kissing under the mistletoe!

The turkey is being basted

While relatives are getting wasted!

Pretty wrapped presents are under the tree

From our loved ones for you and me

A time to give a time to share

A time to tell people how much we care

And as the year comes to an end

This message now I send

To everyone who are so dear

I wish you a Merry Christmas and a Happy New Year!

A Little Sunshine

You bring a little sunshine

to my dark and dreary day

When I get a message from you

and read what you have to say!

It's like the film "You've got Mail"

if anything, this is what I'd compare

Because we both have a lot to give

and also a lot to share

You say I have thoughtful verses

and with intellect I burst

I have an eye for beauty

and a passion for words like thirst

You seemed to have opened me up

and see where my treasures hide

For I can look all around and

absorb things deep inside

Frozen Image

Looking at a picture there is so much to see
Like facing a mirror it's so visible to me

The scene is set back in the olden days
Years ago with their old fashioned ways

Blue skies the sun begins to shine
The greyish brown used railway line

Two boys standing at the hedge's gate
To see the 557 train they eagerly await

The driver mouths a "hello" over to the boys
Who can hardly hear him due to all the noise

Parked in the background a bus and a car

Ready to take passengers near and afar

Little brick built house the white picket fence

A lady sits on the platform upon a wooden bench

White flowered shrubs heathers and ferns

Two silvery coloured metal milk churns

Advertisement displays OXO, Spillers and Camp

Lined on the platform two posts of lantern lamps

Just a picture, a frozen image demonstration

Capturing the artist's vivid imagination

Golden Sands

The sandy beach stretches along for
    miles like a golden strip

Salt is filled in the air and I can taste it
    when I lick my lips

Seagulls together swarm and dart above
    the green clear sea

In search for some food – maybe a fish
    for their tea?

Children bare foot paddle at the edge of
    the sea's shore

Running away from the icy water and
    returning back for more

The sea trickles over castles and
    inscriptions in the sand

Writings and pictures made from adults
    and children's hands

Pebbles on the beach are smooth to
    touch and shiny to the eye

From the sunshine rays and the wash of
    salty water passing by

People disappear and go home as the
    weather turns fair

Leaving the golden sandy beach lonely
    deserted and bare

July to September

You said you never wanted to hurt me,

but I'm hurting now

I know it wasn't your intention or mine

In mind it was just fun

My heart made it something else

My tears wont stop falling

My heart wont stop aching

I've lost something special, it's you

Feel so dead inside

Like a light's gone out

Now I need a drink

To get anywhere from where I am –

"Alone"

No regrets I have, would do it ALL again

Every song I hear reminds me of us, of now,

Some comfort is you felt the same way

Don't feel so empty knowing that

Your words will always stick

Strong for both of us you led on

Never have I wept so much as I have right now

Like my words they have flowed straight from my
heart

I am but alone, no one here to console me

My heart is like a desert

Empty, bare, an illusion that something or someone
is there

Will you ever read these words?

Will you know they are for you?

Will you ever realise how deep I fell for you?

Blinded, myself I did not know

I am the one who seems to be alone

Maybe that's how it's got to be?

Strange, when I have so much love to give?

I'm not bad or heartless or even cold

Why is someone punishing me?

I want to feel better than this...

To have you hold me

Your breath on my lip

Not for anyone – but you

I've never written so free

Yet I need to and I breathe it

FOR IT IS ME

You never questioned why -

You loved me as I was

Please save me I'm drowning -

in my words that flow so easily

Have I written these words?

Do I say these things?

Where are they flowing from?

I hardly know, I guess my heart

Is this the end of the chapter?

Is a new one about to start?

I feel inspired even at the end

I want us to be and believe we can be so much
   more...

My Unborn Child

My doctor told me what I
wanted to hear

That I was pregnant and I
began to cheer

I rushed to tell your daddy who
was full of joy

I told him we'd be having a girl
or a boy!

You start to come active and
give a kick

And in the morning I feel a
little sick

The warm home which
embraces you inside

In my womb I carry you with
enormous pride!

My clothes that I wear are now
rather tight

I crave for pickled gherkins in
the middle of the night!

Going for a scan we both see
you and your heart beat

Every bit of you is perfect
down to your little feet

I am told you are growing at a
steady pace

And I just long to see you and
kiss your little face

Entering this world you let out
an almighty scream

I lie there exhausted, bewildered,
thinking this is all a dream

I hold you in my arms you are
so precious to me

And I whisper to you – you
open your eyes to see

You are tiny and perfect with
ten fingers and ten toes

With some hair, tiny mouth and
a little nose

Daddy has much love for you
it's written on his face

As he holds you tenderly in his
safe embrace

Mummy and daddy came
together and we mated

It's evident to see – a "treasure"
we created

Rainbows

After the rain has been
a rainbow now I've seen
High above in the sky
as below begins to dry

And as the rainbow bends
will I ever reach the end?
Will there be a pot of gold
or is that a fairy tale told?

An endless arch open wide
behind the clouds it hides
Pink, yellow and green shades
now the rainbow begins to fade

I was happy the rainbow was here
but now it's gone away I fear
No rainbow, the sky is plain
but I hope it will visit us again

Romantic Dinner

The scene is set the mood is right

And romance fills the air tonight

Silvery rays shine from the stars and moon

The grand piano playing a delicate tune

Centre posy porcelain vase - a red rose it holds

Linen cloths crisply laden - serviettes in folds

Glass carafe filled with wine red and white

Slender candles burn a flame of golden light

Logs roughly chopped burn on the open fire

Emotions, thoughts and passions of desire

Loving couples seated opposite and dine

Crystal flutes holding champagne or wine

Between starter, main course and maybe an after

The happiness and joyfulness of their laughter

Whispering sweet nothings in each others' ears

Spending the time with the ones they love dear

Summer is here at last!

Summer is here at last during the
   month of June

And the fire ball sun is at its
   hottest around noon

Soaking all the sun our skin
   absorbs the heat

Walking in sandals or nothing on
   our feet

The lawn is laid and green with
   shoots and daisy heads

Whilst decorative borders flush
   with colours of lavenders pinks
   and reds

Children eat ice cream and shade
   themselves to keep cool

Playing water fights and paddling
   in the pool

People around everywhere
   partying and having fun

Eating barbecue food and
   enjoying the sun

And as I apply my skin with
   factor eight

I know that the temperature will
   hold out 'till late

Pollen is collected from the
   flowers by the bumble bees

And birds softly sing whilst
   perched up in the trees

And as a cool air sweeps through
   just a little breeze

It brings with it some pollen and
   I begin to sneeze!

Summer Rain

The wind whistles and moans
The cool breeze freezing my bones

The trees sway and shake
The rippling water of the lake

The heaven opens and lets out rain
And water trickles down the pane

I am safe and have nothing to fear
Now that the rain is finally here

Big spots splashing, making a sound
Wetting and covering the dirty ground

The clouds break, the sky is blue
Sunlight shining, seeking through

The rain dies and there is light
The clouds fluffy and white

The air is warm and clear
Now that the sun is here

The Fifth of November

The air is clear but it is cold on
  this night

The sky black but is lit with an
  orange light

And as I walk closer I can see
  the large fire burn

The firework display is set –
  the Catherine Wheels turn

The smell of smoke fills this
  cold night's air

With adults advising children to
  take extra care

I can smell onions frying and
  hot dogs at a nearby stall

Fireworks explode up in the
  sky and then they fall

Children with sparklers swirl
  them round and round

Silver sparks fly off them
  making a hissing sound

Toffee apples, bonfire toffee
  and candy floss

Rubbish on the fire, the guy is
  nearly lost

Pretty colours of the fireworks
 green, blue and pink

Shooting up in the clear sky
 and then they fade and sink

Children wrapped in hats,
 scarves and gloves

Whilst watching the lit up sky
 above

The last firework leaves the
 display

Now it's all over, this year for
 today

Same expectations, excitement
 and fear

We'll relive the experience
 again next year

The Demon of the Drink!

I wonder why

my mouth is dry

The need to get

something wet

My tongue to soak

a brandy and coke

That went down nice

order again twice

My head feels dizzy

the bubbles are fizzy

More drink please

I feel at ease

Confidence gain

I feel sane

nothing I fear

but you my dear

What do you think?

talking about "the drink"

Too many I have sunk

now I feel quite drunk

The drinks taken over me

like an addiction you see

I start to weep

the urge to sleep

Feeling so sad

my head hurts bad

I've had my kick

now I feel sick

In my mind I think

I've had enough of "the drink"!

Wedding Day

This morning breaks on a high

Sun shining and the blue sky

Today is brilliantly bright

The bride is dressed in white

Groom and his party are all in grey

Upon this happy event – a Wedding Day

The churchyard is littered with folk about

As the church bells begin to bellow out

In the early morning dew

Lilies line the pews

Bride and her father step through the arch

Walking in time to the Wedding March

The congregation in prayer heads bowed

Now the ceremony of the wedding vows

Fragrant smell from the lilies linger

As bands are placed on their fingers

A contract which is made for life

Now they're pronounced "husband and wife"

Tranquil Bliss

With candles flickering flame

And aromatic flavours the room

Seeping from the window

Silvery beams from the moon

Essence of vanilla spice and lavender

Blissfully fulfilling and tranquil

Peaceful calm surroundings

All around is still

Water flows hot and steamy

Bubbles rise and gather

In I step, soaking

I create a lather

Engulfing bubbled water overlaps

Mist dancing in the air

Lying here covered

Dreaming of a place somewhere

Thoughts of a day that's over

A flooding in my mind

Disappearing to nothing

As I start to relax and unwind

Music plays a gentle role

My eyes I start to close

At peace now physically

And within my heart and soul

Up and Away!

The flight number is announced
over the tannoy

And a rush of excitement fulfils
us all with joy

Saving up for months but now I
can afford

As we line up queuing and wait to
climb aboard

With a cheerful smile and a
welcoming greet

Stepping on the plane an air
hostess you meet

Patient, seated and waiting in
anticipation

Eagerly upon this happy duration!

The air hostess points out the
exits and the loos

Then the pilot tells us all the
general flying news

As the aeroplane revs up and
  starts to roll in motion

Air hostesses act out the life
  jacket demonstration

Turbo, boost and thrust, the
  plane belts up the runway

Jetting off the ground upwards
  and away!

Cars like tiny beetles and fields
  are matchbox size

Always getting smaller as the
  plane increases its rise

The view from the window a
  truly wonderful sight

My ears pop from the pressure
  whilst I'm on this flight

A complimentary drink and
  breakfast, dinner or tea

Passing away the time, a little
  pleasure for you and me

A little at a time you can feel the
  plane decrease

My ears from the pressure, the
  pain seems to ease

My tummy begins to somersault
  just a little bit

Eager now to land safely –
  excitedly we sit

The aeroplane's engine makes a
  screeching sound

At last we have touched down -
  the wheels are on the ground!

When our holiday is over after
  ten more nights

I will look forward to flying home
  on our outward flight!

Lost In Thought

I lie here all alone...

The only noise the CD tone

Gentle music plays there

And my skin's tickled by the evening's air

I think of you, though you're not here

As the breeze softly whispers in my ear

My thoughts, emotions running high

So vast like the dark night's sky

You've touched my soul deep within

Filled my heart with love, lust and sin

You're all I need – your love I crave

To be your partner, friend, lover, slave

Like one we fit so neat together

Right now, always and forever

Our hearts beat our souls connect

Strength, friendship, love and intellect

Explosive feelings erupt and burst

You're like a drug I crave your thirst

The breeze whispers your name

And candles flicker its flame

As goose bumps swarm my skin

I shiver from head to toe within

Like your gentle caress I feel

As your prisoner my heart you steal

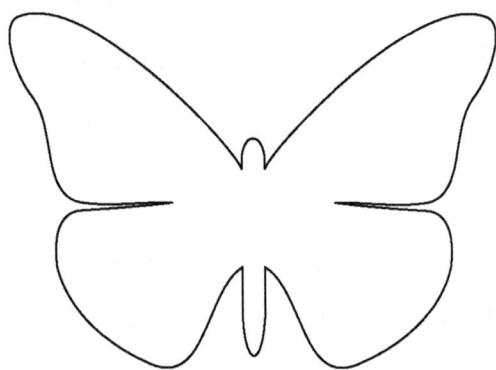

Ready to be taken - I willingly go

As my heart absorbs you so

On a journey through my soul you make

That beats so passionately for you I ache

For over my heart with love you sign

And my search is over, for you are mine

Last Sleep Poem?

I cannot sleep!

If only I could think of counting sheep?

Maybe then sleep would come

And in the morning I would not be dumb

With sleep deprivation I sadly lack

As I lie here on my back!

My yawns are loud and wide

And under the covers here I hide

Thoughts in my head flying around

While everyone else is sleeping sound!

No sleep, no REM, no dreams I sigh

As here alone I lie

Longing and craving for that touch

A need, a want so much

I close my eyes and pray

That sleep engulfs me in every way

My eyes are heavy, my heart so full

Murky waters and like life is dull

Escape dear thoughts and let me sleep

For now I fear I have to weep ...

Our Love

I know you are carried away in sleep

My thoughts of you are way down deep

And my eyes start to leak

As tears tumble down my cheek

The romantic film has touched my heart

And it makes me think of us apart

It gives me a warm glow

For me now, for what I know

That love is all around

Like rich colours and melancholic sounds

And what joy I absorb when I think of thee

In what we could have and all we could be

A sense of belonging and also free

For you are YOU and I am ME

So now down my head I lie

With thoughts of you this nigh'

Whether we are apart or together as two

I know that you love me and I love you

Who You Are

Always be who you are -

whether that is good or bad

You are not in a play here -

life is not an act

If someone does not like you -

for whom you really are

Then they do not deserve you -

and you should distance yourself
afar

Mistrust and hurt -

even I have been there

When tears have uncontrollably
fallen -

it did not seem fair

Seems like everyone sometimes -

wants to take and never give

It is like people have gone mad -

in this crazy world we live

I treat others -

like I wish to be

Only then can I be happy -

with me

So cast aside -

your troublesome past

And make this a relationship of
    friendship -

to last

Forbidden?

I express no concerns really but only for
    this

That what I am experiencing is utter
    sweet bliss

Your words are written deeply and I
    know what you feel

Like a deep cut I bleed your words to
    me heal

Your passion is strong and also quite
    hidden

But like a flower you open more it's not
    so forbidden

You appear somehow guarded or even a
    little shy

Like you have been hurt bad and your
    heart been bruised by

We all have that baggage, all been used
    in some way

Even though that seems sad it is the
    truth which I say

Do not get gloomy you are like a breath
    of fresh air

I am pleased you messaged me because
    for you I do care

Awake

You are in my life it's me you found

I'm longing for your arms around

Here at night locking the door

Cuddled one another safe and secure

Your gentle kiss

Is what I miss

As here I lie alone

Like no emptiness I have known

On the bed foetal curled

While traffic noise from the outside world

Prevented from sleep my feelings here

My thoughts of you my dear

And you will not hear my joyful cries

I try for sleep and close my eyes

I will drift through R E M

And I will see you then

Anything to me in my dreams

To work it out what all this means

My heart is heavy and full

For on my heartstrings you do pull

Time...

Upon the shelf the clock fits neatly

As its hands tick away so discreetly

Another day passes sometimes fast

One second later the other be past

Time passes slow in the build up to our meeting

But hours roll into days after our first greeting

Storing precious moments up in our mind

Like being enveloped together entwined

Engulfing me like a protective cover

I feel the warmth of you, my lover

Like an ocean deep and vast

As if a love-spell over me you cast

Our days spent - where did they go?

Too fast to catch and freeze time to slow

Your embrace is wanton your heart full

My overall existence soul you pull

Out of reach of caresses of lips

Of touches of slight finger tips

Abandoned of holds so dear

Of heart beats I feel when near

We long for another day – when we will be

Together again, in love, just you and me

Winter Nights

Candles on the hearth burn

Winter Nights alone

Gentle music softly plays

Outside the wind whistles and groans

All curled up on the sofa

Locking the world away

Hot mug of cocoa

Ending another day

Thoughts and feelings slipping

Erasing from my mind

Comfortable I sit

Slowly I unwind

Darkness engulfs the room

Swallows deep inside

Safe I am in here

All alone I hide

Contented in myself

I am secure and sound

Feelings of being loved

Overwhelms me all around

War Destruction and Peace

I think the world is going to crumble

When in the night I hear a rumble

It is planes I hear throughout the night

They seem very loud and out of sight

Too much talk of war and destruction

Like we are awaiting for an eruption

The newsflashes of those who are dead

In my heart the fear and dread

It can happen here the whole world to its knees

No to surrender no time to pack and leave

Like a cold rush I feel it is coming

Nowhere to hide we can do no running

I pray that someday the world will have peace

Violence and power be on a decrease

No wars any more no fighting I crave

Whatever will be I try to be brave

To have if only to love one another

The closeness of sister and brother

Too many sacrifices too many graves

Hope this world we live in can be saved

And if there is a God above

Please shine through and bring us love

For now I put my hands together and pray

That peace will be in our world one day

Think Positively!

You are feeling unhappy and sad

Sometimes when your life is bad

Seeing a rainbow makes you smile

You have not felt like that in a while

The weather is dark and dim

And your life is feeling grim

But you are alive today

So make the most of it in every way

Pain in your heart you cannot bear

Things seem to be really unfair

Try to be positive in the things you do

And in the end all will come right for you

When you are down and crying inside

And all you want to do is run and hide

There is some friend with an ear to lend

To bridge a gap to make amends

Sometimes you feel all alone

Leaving you to moan and groan

Instead try to sing a little song

Indeed it will do no wrong

Chaos and harsh words scream

Releasing off your steam

Let it be peaceful and calm

It would not do any harm

Hurting with verbal and physical blow

Makes you not want to stay but go

To this person you really should care

Not try to maim, frighten or scare

When you are down and out

And feel the need to shout

STOP! And think life is great

Takes too much effort to HATE

Blue skies and the sun will be out again

For a while there will be no more rain

Positively for you this will be a new start

And you will be happy again in your heart

Poppies

A cottage stands alone

With its old sandy stone

The orangey sun beats down

Colours mingled upon the ground

Everything is calm and mellow

Wheat and barley corn of yellow

Poppies lie upon their bed

A mass of sea of red

Like a swarm of bees they stay

And in the breeze they sway

Delightfully they spring and dance

Breathtaking to see them at a glance

A flower so pretty yet just a weed

So eager to spread its seed

Prettiness lines grass verges

In fields overtakes and merges

On Remembrance Day the poppy is worn

For soldiers who fought and died in the war

Unforgotten graves yet covered with moss

The poppy flower marks their cross

Its appearance elegant and fine

The poppy is a favourite of mine

A poppy field is such a special find

I picture it and store it in my mind

Peaceful Waters

The setting is tranquil –
all asleep and still

'Peaceful Waters' calm -
free from any harm

Sparkling sapphire of blue -
away the birds have flew

Empty above the boat -
balancing and afloat

Indigo and violet skies -
pretty sunsets and sunrise

It could be anywhere -
but not a place I share

And until I depart -
it is locked inside my heart

For when I am here -
there is nothing I fear

Like waters of the sea -
emotions released are free

This is a love of grace -
my 'Peaceful Waters' place

Good Friends

You can have good friends which I've had

Ones who make you happy when you are sad

Someone you can rely on to be true

When you are feeling lonely and blue

A good friend is truly hard to find

When the two of you bond and bind

In thick and thin they stick to you like glue

Just to help you see your way through

A shoulder to cry on, a listening ear

They comfort and support you sincere

If the tables were turned you would do the same

Seeing your friend happy would be your aim

When you are mixed up and in some strife

They will offer you advice along the path of life

Such good friends around to care

With problems we all need to share

Sometimes life is hard when we need to make
  amends

But where would we be without our good friends?

Dear Santa

I write this letter Santa, to you so very
dear

To tell you I have been a good girl all
throughout the year

I have behaved well and help my
mum when I can

I try to be a loving sister to my little
brother, Dan

I hope your sack is chock-a-block full
of nice big toys

Enough to go all around the girls and
the boys

I will leave my stocking here and hope
that you will fill

And place them on the sofa in case
they overspill!

A carrot I leave for Rudolph, for you
a glass of sherry

Hoping that it warms your belly but
doesn't make you merry

I will write again next year and will be
  good for mum and dad

Because you don't give toys to
  children naughty or bad

Up the chimney now you go back into
  your sleigh

And you will visit every house before
  the break of day

In the cold black sky the twinkling
  stars shine so bright

Rudolph leads your sleigh flying you
  through the night

Inside presents wrapped big and small
  in paper lie around

As the magic of Christmas is here and
  fresh snow covers the ground

An April Day –
Farewell Grandad

It was warm and sunny seemed a
   perfect day

But upsetting for us all as you leave
   to go away

Family greet us and we try to be
   strong

You do not come to see us – this
   feels so wrong

When I see you resting there my
   eyes start to leak

Feel guilty I am hurting I wipe the
   tears from my cheek

I lose a feeling within and crave to
   be alone

The stream is tranquil and I
   imagine you like stone

We act well for others but really
   our hearts are aching

And when we are alone we know
   our hearts are breaking

Things you loved in life are there
   in death too

Because everyone around, was
   really fond of you

People came from near and far
  with their respects to pay

To the rest of the world ... it was
  just another day

And it is funny that life goes on yet
  WE feel so sad

It is like a crazy situation like the
  world has gone mad

The heavens open and let out rain

Maybe from God to ease our pain?

With no hope of return you leave

And we start on our path to grieve

The soldiers line up just for you
  and I start to cry

Or is it the rain trickling down my
  face I don't know why

We sit in rows I can smell the
  wood of the pew

Like the fresh dampness from the
  morning's dew

The hymns we sing or hum, who is
actually singing?

Sounds like church bells so
brilliantly ringing

The vicar starts his speech and a
poem I wrote so dear

And we weep uncontrollably as we
see you disappear

People give good wishes – they are
so kind

I just think it is all surreal like it is
all in my mind

We toast and eat to you and your
good life

And trust that you are now with
your wife

We were, and are of you very fond

And we will always have a special
bond

You are in our hearts with
Grandma together

And we will never forget, we will
love you forever

www.ingramcontent.com/pod-product-compliance
Lightning Source LLC
Chambersburg PA
CBHW060939040426
42445CB00011B/924